Finding the Edge

by

Al Ortolani

WOODLEY MEMORIAL PRESS

Contents

Introduction

Finding the Edge

Finding the Edge *3*
On a Brighter Note the Christmas Lights Are Up *4*
The Poet Stranded in West Texas *5*
Dropping the Old Elm *6*
After Hard Times, Lazarus Feel the Beginning of Something Good *7*
Good Friday *8*
A Young Poet Brings Her Teacher Flowers *9*
The Teacher Drifts into Daydream *10*
strawberry as verb *11*
Alone in Mexico, the Poet Resorts to Love Poems *12*
In Spring Storm *13*
In Search of Huevo Rancheros *14*
As if War Was Inevitable, Wally Decides to Test the Secret Weapon *15*
The Generous Woman *16*
The Crow and the Cloud *17*
Frisbee Investigates the Angle of Love *18*
New Beginning Car Wash *19*
A Lesson about the Bonks *20*

Strip Mine Resurgence

Summer Storm Among the Strip Pits *23*
After Graduation Wally Rummages in the Strip Pits *24*
A Strip Mine Resurgence *25*
The Petrified Cowboy *26*
The Dupe *27*
Nighthawks *28*
Boxed In *29*
Breathing Cave *30*
Alice Cracks the Toilet While Singing
            Old Rock and Roll Top 40 Hits *31*
The Junkyard Mechanic Finds His Voice *32*
We Find Ourselves with Frogs *33*
The Two Directions of a Drone *34*
Recipe for Change *35*
Cleaning Out the Garage *36*
Burning the Beans while Meditating *37*

Bonnie the Clover Lady *38*
Mama DeBeauty Explains a Necessary But Uncomfortable
                    Aspect of Dude Ranching *39*
Water Strider *41*
Vienna Sausage *42*

Game Prayer

Game Prayer *45*
Losing Our Paychecks at Bocci *46*
A Kansan Visits New York City *47*
Coyotes *48*
In Search of Five Mile Cave *49*
Hunting the Oldest Grave in the Town Cemetery *50*
Shooting the Snapper *51*
The Last Bones of Mine Creek *52*
The Oxbow *53*
Hiking with the Cedar Children *54*
Rappelling Out of El Ojo Del Gato in Cloud Cover *55*
Satori in a Village in Old Mexico *56*
"How St. Anthony Converted the Heretics
                by Preaching to the Fishes" *57*
The Day Before Winter *58*

Reading to Her Daughter

Hunting New Cave on Cecil Creek *61*
Wintered Bat at John Eddy Cave *62*
Some Moments Are Frozen *63*
Muskrat Dump *64*
Walking Pine Creek in Winter *65*
The Something Above Which We Share Below *66*
How Wally Lost His Thumb and the Boy Scouts Became Cannibals *67*
Double Dating with Wally *69*
The Great Night with Rednecks *71*
Anything for Susie *72*
Puttering *74*
Copperhead *75*
The Night of Bacon and Baseball *76*
Maybe if Kafka *77*
Make Believe Indian Love Poem *78*
Where a deer fell *79*
Reading to Her Daughter *80*

Acknowledgements

The author wishes to thank the editors of the following journals in which many of these poems, sometimes in different versions, first appeared.

Aethlon: The Journal of Sport Literature: "Game Prayer"

Bellowing Ark: "Muskrat Dump", "Bonnie the Clover Lady", "Breathing Cave", "Lazarus Feels the Beginning of Something Good", "On a Brighter Note, the Christmas Lights Are Up"

Coal City Review: "Losing Our Paychecks at Bocci", "A Lesson about the Bonks"

Earthwise Newsletter: "Song of Rivers", "Reading to Her Daughter"

The English Journal: "How Wally Lost His Thumb and the Boy Scouts Became Cannibals"

Hocked Gun Press Broadside: "Coyotes", "Satori in a Village in Old Mexico"

Kansas English: "Wintered Bat at John Eddy Cave", "Puttering", "A Summer Storm Among the Strip Pits", "Nighthawks", "The Generous Woman"

Kansas Voices: "Finding the Edge"

The Laurel Review: "Two Directions of a Drone"

Little Balkans Review: "Hiking with the Cedar Children", "The Day Before Winter", "In Spring Storm"

The Midwest Quarterly: "The Junkyard Mechanic Finds His Voice", "The Oxbow", "A Strip Mine Resurgence"

Modern Haiku: "The School Teacher Drifts into Daydream"

Present Magazine.Com: "Boxed In", "Cleaning Out the Garage", "Copperhead", "The Crow and the Cloud", "Dropping the Old Elm", "How St. Anthony Converted the Heretics by Preaching to the Fishes", "Maybe if Kafka", "The Poet Stranded in West Texas", "Recipe for Change", "In Search of Five Mile Cave"

Poetry Motel: "Some Moments Are Frozen"

The Piedmont Literary Review: "A Young Poet Brings Her Teacher Flowers", "Make Believe Indian Love Poem"

The Quarterly: "Double Dating with Wally", "Frisbee Investigates the Angle of Love", "Mama DeBeauty Explains a Necessary But Uncomfortable Aspect of Dude Ranching", "The Dupe", "The Something Above Which We Share Below"

The Redneck Review of Literature: "Alone in Mexico the Poet Resorts to Love Poems", "In Search of Huevo Rancheros"

The Sow's Ear Poetry Review: "Rappelling Out of El Ojo Del Gato in Cloud Cover"

Wilderness: "Hunting New Cave on Cecil Creek", "Walking Pine Creek in Winter", "Where a deer fell"

The Windless Orchard: "Water Strider"

"Hunting New Cave on Cecil Creek" and "Where a deer fell" were anthologized in *Wild Song: Poems of the Natural World*, edited by John Daniel and published by *The University of Georgia Press*.

"Finding the Edge", winner of the *Kansas Voices Poetry Contest* of Winfield, Kansas.

"A Strip Mine Resurgence" was selected for *The Midwest Quarterly: 50th Anniversary Poetry Issue*, 100 Poems from 50 Years, edited by Stephen Meats.

"A Kansas Visits New York City" was included in *150 Kansas Poems, Celebrating Kansas' Sesquicentennial*, edited by Caryn Mirriam-Goldberg.

Woodley Press
Washburn University
Topeka, Kansas 66621

Author's Note

I would like to thank the following editors, friends and family, who in the course of the writing of these poems, have lent their support, criticism and creative eye:

Editors and Wordsmiths: Robert Day, Gene DeGruson, Michael Heffernan, Dan Jaffe, Gordon Lish, Jo McDougall, Stephan Meats and William Trowbridge.

The Editorial Staff of *The Little Balkans Review*: Chris Blancho, Wayne Bockelman, Tom Burns, Mike Hogard, John Laflen, James Ortolani and Trent Stern;

White Buffalo Poetry and Blues: Adam Jameson, J.T. Knoll, and Lem Sheppard;

The Armadillo Chili Medicine Show, The Brick Mountain Players, Picasso Brothers Painting, Terry Collins, Skip McConnell, Dana Cope, Steve Eichhorn and Debra Waldorf;

Woodley Press, Editor, Dennis Etzel, Jr.;

Ron Michael, Curator, Birger Sandzen Memorial Gallery, in Lindsborg, Kansas;

"Thomas Merton." BrainyQuote.com. Xplore Inc, 2011. 5 January. 2011. http://www.brainyquote.com/quotes/quotes/t/thomasmert120697.

Likewise, thanks to my students who over the past 37 years have given meaning and purpose to my life, and, of course, my family: my parents Al and Virginia Ortolani; my children Karissa and Blane Reeves, Theresa and Wes Middleton, Tyler Allen and Staci Allen; the newest additions, Jack, Ava and Rider; and finally to my loving wife, Sherri, to whom this volume is dedicated.

And let me not forget Wally, wherever and whenever he may turn up.

Introduction

I am thankful and honored to introduce this collection of Al Ortolani's work. Almost two decades ago, Woodley Press published his book of poems The Last Hippie of Camp 50, so I was pleased that he offered this collection to us. Some might know him as a teacher, others as an editor for Little Balkans Review. I want everyone to know he is a true poet of craft and endurance.

As a reader of ecopoetry, I enjoyed this wonderful collection. Ortolani is a poet of place, including how culture feeds that place. Kansas is here. So is the Southwest, Mexico, and a visit to New York. He uses the imagery of place as a means of connection. As the speaker of the poem connects with an emotional state, so does the reader:

> like a child whose guardian angel //
> has slipped from heaven
> and perched like a yellow bird on the bedstead,
> meadowlarks
> rising from fence posts ("After Hard Times...")

This is ecopoetry—the kind that connects the reader back to the natural world through the poet's observations. Several poems in this collection do this, like "We Find Ourselves with Frogs": "A frog's world / must be one of sudden change, expanding / the way they do to find lovers." There are caves to explore, coyotes to find.

Culture is also found in these pages—lost cultures rediscovered. One sequence in this concentrates on the strip mines and its effect on the environment and place. The poem "After Graduation Wally Rummages in the Strip Pits..." is a wonderful list poem that uncovers, as much as it recovers, the cultural artifacts that are buried with a hint of the turmoil of the times.

Another thing I enjoy is Ortolani's sense of humor in his work—something I appreciate when I find it in poetry. Read through this collection and you will find a wonderful balance of humor with reflection, discovery with irony. The trick to being humorous is in subtlety, which is what I enjoyed in the following:

> Among an ancestral people, he imagines
> he would have been the one
> called upon to put names to the unknown,
> to find in the indifference of stars
> a message above the mesa.

> However, today
> needs to rebuild the carburetor with the tools at hand:
> a roll of duct tape, a library card and an audio book
> on the taming of the American West. ("The Poet
> Stranded in West Texas")

I had to chuckle about the modern dilemma in this poem. We all wish to connect with the mysticism that other places outside of cities provide, including sacred places. However, we sometimes just want to get home.

In a way, these poems do this—take us into an ecology: a study of home. There are poems of childhood (find Wally in several poems), of finding home in the environment, and in the power of language:

> Her daughter listens, and in the end
> will touch her fingers to her mother's lips
> like a willow twig dragging current,
> language breaking around her   ("Reading to Her
> Daughter")

Ultimately, "Finding the Edge" becomes its own metaphor. This title poem gives us a clue to how we should have trust, and hold on to those glimpses of fully trusting in: a beloved who leads us to "the edge" and holds on, the natural world just at the edge of what is "civilization," or in language, where poetry begins at the edge of where the literal ends.

Get ready to set out for a poetic adventure.

Thank you, Al!

Dennis Etzel Jr.
November 2010

for Sherri

Finding the Edge

Finding the Edge

You put both hands over my eyes
and walked me, scuffing leaves
through the hardwoods,
until we emerged into a clearing
unspeckled by cooling shade.

You clamped your fingers tighter
over my eye sockets, and we edged
toe to heel
up over the lens of caprock, limestone

scraping my soles. In the distance
a crow raked the silence, beating winds
filled my hair, and punched my jacket
with balloons of air.
More you said, a little, a little
and we inched, you nudging my foot
forward like a doorstop.

Then you said look and turned loose your hands.
I blinked,
wobbling on the cliff's edge, gasping at how
the tips of my sneakers extended over the sycamores
two hundred feet below.

I rocked, swaying forward with the reel of gravity,
and I felt the tug of your hand
bunched in the middle of my jacket,
pulling me back, gently
from the treetops, which deceptive in their
bright net of leaves
were rigidly individual, defined
as clearly as the single hawk
quivering in wind drafts.

On a Brighter Note, the Christmas Lights Are Up

I climb the pea pitch roof
and tack a string of white lights
to the peak. In the surrounding air,
the night spreads from my fingertips

to the edge of the continent.
I am touched by the vast Atlantic,
an ocean of blue midnight
that washes my heart in waves

while the lights of shrimp boats
twinkle white on the sea.
I think Christ would smile,
balancing the rigging in bare feet,

his arms wide, spread in salt spray.
Tonight, we unwind large nets,
buoyed in the darkness of rooftops,
a string of lights, bright

as baskets of fish.

The Poet Stranded in West Texas

Odd blue lizards and a goosey wind
rattle through the greasewood.
The poet whose car has died on a back road to Santa Fe,
unnerved by the remoteness of the water tank,

examines the towns he has circled
on his map of the panhandle. The more he studies
the more they begin to look like constellations.
In the rearview mirror, it reads
"All truths are closer than they appear."

Among an ancestral people, he imagines
he would have been the one
called upon to put names to the unknown,
to find in the indifference of stars
a message above the mesa.

                    However, today
he needs to rebuild the carburetor with the tools at hand:
a roll of duct tape, a library card and an audio book
on the taming of the American West.

Dropping the Old Elm

The sawyer spots the fall
the way you'd lick your thumb
and then smear spit

on your forehead. This place
and he nods towards the lawn
between two outbuildings

is where she'll topple. He
slips a silver dollar from
his baggy jeans and marks

the fall, lays it on the grass
like a wager. It's all
in the angle of the notch

carved into the trunk, horizontal
as a question, and then a rip downwards
in a rough forty-five, so the two cuts

join like an answer.
If there's no limbs or high
wires or sudden whimsy of wind

to mar the trajectory,
she'll drop, forty years of swaying,
second guessing onto the dollar.

After Hard Times, Lazarus Feels
the Beginning of Something Good

He has driven all night
and can find no rest. He thinks
of himself as Lazarus risen
but not quite alive,

calls himself that name
in idle conversations with the windshield,
poems to the radio knobs that glow
in green iridescence.

He has crossed Kansas in rain
and with dawn is steering into the
watery veins of eastern fields.
Any moment, the sun

will drop a single rope
from between blue clouds, and he
will dance on the wet highway
like a child whose guardian angel

has slipped from heaven and perched
like a yellow bird on the bedstead,
meadowlarks rising from fence posts.

Good Friday

I've worried all night how to save
the cardinal from bashing
his brainpan against the window.

Three days he has been battling
behind the barberry
to nest and feed. His other self

arrives as he does, uncanny
in his ability to surface in glass,
to dispute the twigs and fragments of string.

He descends in a nervous flutter,
his warfare rapping into the silent house
like a knuckle at the basement window.

I shroud the window with duct tape
and brown grocery sacks, fighting the gas meter,
squatting off balance in the cedar chips.

The thorny briars bleeding
my shirt like cat claws.

A Young Poet Brings Her Teacher Flowers

She tossed him a bouquet of daisies,
wrapped in green florist's paper.
"I have picked you flowers.

Picked them from among a field of wildflowers
in the FTD showcase." In poetry
it's the thing that counts.

Words float off
like milkweed fuzz,
settling acres away among susans

so numerous we become lost to them.
Within a poem, the right line
can loft above our heads

like fluff in wind currents.
When she throws her teacher daisies,
he spins, leaps across his desk

and catches poems,
holds them up to sun
in a Pepsi bottle vase.

The Teacher Drifts into Daydream

The first dandelions have broken ground and wave their yellow crowns above the turning Bermuda. I've brought my classes outdoors for a few minutes of writing. Free writing I've called it. I won't worry about the product. My attention wanders.

> Drifting the canoe
>   in honeysuckle shade,
>   a hummingbird's light

I looked up the word morose today in Webster's and found that it has to do with tendencies towards gloom and melancholy. The phrase spring fever reoccurs frequently in the hallways. A boy on the far bench folds his arm across his eyes and reclines in the sun. He drifts with wind currents.

> Abandoned fishing cabin,
>   Virginia creeper netting
>   a row of catfish heads

By mid-period my head is so heavy that I can't focus my eyes. Conversations swirl and sputter as if fragmented by sudden whirlpools. My canoe pushes away from shore. The river is still and deep, bottled by a fallen ash.

> The plop of paddle blade
>   dips ash leaf mold, whirlpools
>   swirl away in the heat

Below the keel, schools of pebble colored shad dart upstream. For no apparent reason, they all turn in unison towards a willow jungle. I cannot help but wonder what signal was given.

> Between watercress
>   the mountain spring
>   flows out of darkness

My class has quieted. They've folded notebooks behind their heads and are counting clouds, or face down, turned on stomachs, they gaze into the folds of dandelions, the creases of wild lettuce, the shadows of clover. Somewhere a lawn mower drones.

strawberry as verb

a blank page is like early spring
when there is little
yet to name, and even less
with which to punctuate the hills

few nouns, invisible adjectives,
little growth,
yet, still there is movement,
a deep churning
in root and bulb and warming seed

so like the white flower
of the wild strawberry,
a poem is found
in connection
from root to leaf
of green

from runner to runner
igniting spring

as from pen to paper
a noun vibrates
to verb

Alone in Mexico, the Poet Resorts to Love Poems

He takes the last poem, the one
that will turn a certain woman's head
or make the whole world cry,
and admires the flow of the bluest ink
in Mexico. Then, to deliver
the poem
he hires a goat
and ties the paper below his scruffy neck

with a blue bandana. Slapping
the goat's skinny ass,
he shoos it on towards the border.
"My future depends upon that poem,
you silly cabrito,
so when you cross the river

keep your neck high. Travel only at night.
Avoid barbeques."

In Spring Storm

In Santa Fe, the houses are of adobe
and some, surrounded by high walls,
have gardens within,
where purple wisteria climbs
and drops a vine over the brown clay
to the sidewalk below.

The bare flesh of my fingers reddens in the gray wind
as I reach for you
through one thousand miles of rain.

In Search of Huevo Rancheros

It is dusk and there is an entire
night to cross before morning.
A single red pickup flips on its headlights
and slides across the mesa.

Two men drive into a mountain of clouds
the color of plums.
Possibly, they are reading Chinese poetry
the yellow light of the cab

like a raft on the Yangtze,
or possibly, they are two crows,
hooded and silent,
in love
with nothing but corn.

As if War Was Inevitable, Wally Decides
to Test the Secret Weapon

Wally knew we were coming
stalking diagonally up
the branches, testing and
twisting through the leaves
to the tree house where
he waited on the plywood platform.
When we got halfway,
he stood
and peed, the yellow
stream splattering
above our heads, spraying
off the branches onto
our hands and arms
and faces. We screamed,
slipping down the
way we'd come like insects
in a rain. A heavy
deluge caught Mike
between the shoulder blades,
splattering his T-shirt
like machine gun fire.
Mike fell
dropping into a pile of
discarded lumber.
Wally pinched his last
three squirts in our
direction. We held
close to the main trunk,
the yellow fire streaming
over our heads. Bill
slipped and hung by one hand,
his knuckles white
and beaded with yellow.
It works Wally hollered.
and the boys cheered.

The Generous Woman

When a woman hangs lights
above the entrance to a cave
and then refuses to charge
a single admission,

it says something. Makes free
a statement about what
can be owned and parceled out
like seats at a baseball game,

but it's also just a shade crazy
to be driving in the hills
somewhere between truth and consequence
and discover these multicolored

bulbs submerged in the trees.
It makes you wonder what she
wants you to see, alive and bare
against the hillside.

The Crow and the Cloud

In the deep silence before storm
a hiker leans on a wooden staff.
Rain drops melt into his rag wool
the way a crow cawing in cloud cover

melts into sycamores.
There is a doe in the honeysuckle
and within the body of the doe
is a woman from his past.
She stares at him through brown eyes.

He knows this because of the way
she bolts into the darkness of the evergreens
and in the way his eyes linger
on the canopy of branches

and in the way the crow follows.

Frisbee Investigates the Angle of Love

When Frisbee's girlfriend
chose a woman to be her lover
instead of him,
he flipped
and took to driving
over to Galena and
jumping off of the chat
piles. He had a mathematical mind

and could calculate
the number of bounces
it would take
to keep
a fall from killing him.

He'd jump without fanfare,
unceremoniously,
slowing his descent
by bouncing
from ridge to ridge,

scuffing the gravel
into dozens of scraping
avalanches,
with all of us
looking on as silently
as plants,
assuming he'd lost
his mind as well as
his cherry,

in awe how that girl
must have been one soft cookie
to create

such a crumbling,
setting him up
to climb again
to the lip of the slope and,
before jumping, to mumble aloud,

"Maybe, I'll get it right this time."

New Beginning Car Wash

At the New Beginning Car Wash
Mary and Joseph
look for a spot free rinse for their old Pontiac.
It's a rust bucket

straight from a Judean low-credit lot.
One owner the salesman had said
and Joseph had bartered and haggled
and then paid

in hard earned carpenter's wages.
He had to get his family to Egypt
for danger was in the air
and angels were rattling his dreams.

It is a dusty drive he was thinking
and we are in such a press
what with all this Antipas trouble.
Of course, a car that's newly washed

won't run any better than a dirty one,
but the white walls when scrubbed
will look like halos in the sun
spinning across the Sinai.

A Lesson about the Bonks

One day on lunch duty the principal
Presses up to me
And says, well now I've seen it all,
The two Bonk boys,
Absent all morning, have just arrived
In time for their free or reduced lunch. Watch them
Disappear before the next bell rings.
Mom and dad
Are both sitting outside in the car.

It's a cycle
The way families move in this part of the county,
Just ahead of the bill collectors. The Bonks
Will be gone next month
And we won't see them again
Until spring or fall. I can't blame the kids
For the dumb ass parents who raise them, but then
Do you blame the parents or the dumb ass grandparents
Who raised the parents,
Or for that matter, there's the great grandparents…
The cycle needs broken,
And you young teacher
Straight out of college with the bachelor's degree
Have got to snap it.
Add some literacy.
Teach the Bonks to read,
You've got maybe two months.

A Strip Mine Resurgence

Summer Storm Among the Strip Pits

I have parked on a dump that overlooks
the water. Kingfishers slap surface,
dip and cut wide figure eights, lifting

like flapping hands into the sky.
Rain comes, peppering the surface
like thousands of winged insects, tapping

light fingers against the roof of my van.
Curtains blow. From the tops of poplars
I hear the wind moan, turning the alkali

over upon itself, the clay mixing
with gray shale, trickling
down from the tailings. The small soil

that runs between roots of a willow
clouds the vacant water
and spreads like the spawn of fish.

After Graduation Wally Rummages in the Strip Pits

He finds bonfires and bedsprings,
Windowpane and chains,
peas and carrots, cans opened, dumped
with lids awry. Rabbit fur and wind,
a cat on a trailer hitch. Lost

love, found love, love unopened. Dumped:
redemption, exemption, conscription, lawful dodging,
pectorals and biceps, anarchy and demagogues,
high spirits and rebar. Vietnam. *Crime*

and Punishment, War and Peace, Playboy,
war paint, lacquered fruit, poetry, cabinet drawers stripped
of hardware, gutted for the kitchen of dreams. Nothing
and everything sewn in a coat lining. Flying
monkeys stoned on poppies, a scarecrow, a tin man,
a lion, monopolized. Dorothy clicking her heels.

A prayer rug frayed and threadbare, legs tucked,
twisted in half lotus: sweat socks, jungle boots,
pits of alkaline, fishing line, chicken bones,
stink-bait, jail-bait and maiden-head,
draft card, milkweed and thistles. Kingfishers swinging
figure eights in an open sky. Kite string. Boots
without strings, tampons with strings, walking
on a string, promises as strings. Dragonflies
on wing. Flight. No strings attached.
The lottery: number 69.

Oily rainbows, old dogs without collars, work
without play. The beginning and the end fixed
like a fish knife, a bayonet. St. Christopher,
St. Anthony, St. Jude. (Every home
with a forwarding address.) St. Francis,
Sister Clare. A weekend with Buddhists.
Plywood, cattails, and rust,
herons and cranes and cactus spines.

A boy peering through bullet holes in a stop sign.

A Strip Mine Resurgence

In her charcoal a catfish
wallows in the shallows,
curved like a gurka
and knifed between arrowhead plant
and water lilies.
The afternoon sunlight flattens
a warm plastic sky
stippled with dragonflies.
The artist sits on a shoal of slag,
Tevas splattered with grainy muck,
notebook on her knees.
Each sketch is young with contradiction,
heron wings and beer cans,
glittering glass, a fishing line,
kingfishers
darting against the pit water.

A wand of cane, a cattail
caught by a blackbird, the chocolate
shine of the water turtle's shell
shimmers like a window of wavy glass
and she is pulled by the heat
into a languor, her charcoal
fading along the edges of the paper
into a sort of haze, the heat
smoothing sharp lines and softening
the morning's muscle. Suddenly,
she is lifting her Peruvian skirt
and wading into
the reflection of cottonwoods
cool against her thighs.

The Petrified Cowboy

Death had not reached them
standing at the edge of the carnival
between the reptile tank and the two headed calf.
The boys were unspent,
feeling lucky and new,
as if they held the one ball that could
topple the proverbial three bottles.

It was this unused and unspoken self
that drew them to the tent where the dead cowboy lay,
encased in glass, more a manikin
than a man, claw hands,
sewn eyes, skin shriveled and shining like a wallet.

Ten cents.

The barker shuffled them in and let them gape, railing
about Texas deserts, Egyptian mummies and high mountain caves
but refusing to let them lift the glass. Afterwards
they sat below the city oaks,
confused by the price of truth.
They batted acorns with a stick,
pretending baseball,
popping called shots into the green pond.

The Dupe

You find Babe's bat in a flea market,
authenticated by a reliable source
and priced right, an extravagance
you can afford.
You hang it
on the wall at home,
holding it in times of crises.

Even though your game
was never baseball,
you wax your hands
along its sanded grip,
gradually gaining control of the moment,
clenching your fingers
for the shot,
the one that Ruth called
after two strikes

and put

exactly over the wall
where he'd pointed.

Nighthawks

Inside your body is a wish
when on hot summer nights
you pull a mattress
through the window and lie
like a smoldering cigarette
on the rubberized roof.
Something inside
wants to reverse gravity,
to unpin,
and spin away
weightless from the city.

Inside your body is a wish
that joins with nighthawks
beyond the coaxial cables,
stainless flues and smudges of neon,
beyond the dizzying spires
of steeple and antenna
where street lights fog
and supper clubs
wisp away like smoke.

Inside your body
white streaked wings beat
up from your chest,
your throat, your mouth,
and plunge through your teeth,
releasing from the dry crackle
of skin and bone

your spark.

Boxed In

Inside the cardboard
beside the patio fence,
the small, wire-necked
turtle, rescued

from the passing lane
on US 69, scratches
and claws against
the fibers of the box.

I hear him clearly
above the hedge clippers
that whir among
the manicured shrubs.

After dark, I drive
the roadside down Drywood Creek.
Stopping among the cattails,
I lift him from his

beer-box, moonlit nails
clawing the night air,
straining for the freedom
of wild onion and sage.

For a moment,
after he has pushed
between the reeds and grasses,
I listen for some

tumbling of the stream,
the owl call, the deer
that jumps the fence
downstream.

Breathing Cave

When you sit in the creek bed, training
your headlamp, boots wedged
like mussels amid the new stones,

the cave's breath sneaks to you,
snakes around your legs and pushes
into the lungs of you hiking shorts.

There is a love in her eyes today
that you cannot comprehend
like that afternoon of monarchs

when the long silences began to unwind
and emerge with orange wings.
Still, there is a hesitation.

A deep mist licks the limestone
and slickens the willow's roots
yellow in the evening air.

The crescendo of cicadas thickens
as we enter new passage
trying a foothold, tasting the darkness.

Alice Cracks the Toilet
While Singing Old Rock and Roll Top 40 Hits

Maybe it was coincidence
rather than the pitch and crescendo
of her voice, or maybe

it was more the way she
squirmed and rocked
to scat the right

Joplin note. The harmony came
from her cousin Sal, who
joined her in the bathtub,

perched on the porcelain rim,
leaning towards Alice
who leaned towards Sal,

bongo-ing their fists &
drumming their feet. Even
the toilet paper fluttered

and the medicine cabinet's
supply of cold pills
chattered like castanets

in plastic bottles.
In the end they knew
they had something:

Alice's dad pounding on the door,
mom howling from the kitchen sink,
the cat in hiding

like a caesura.

The Junkyard Mechanic Finds His Voice

He tried to sing,
to release the music that welled up inside
like a clouding seltzer. But when his mouth opened,

scrap iron grated across pickup beds.
He grew still, confused by his awkwardness,
shied like a lizard

and fell back into the bottle, retreating
into the shadows of the yard lamp.
He drew an eye upon the others

who sang in the mercury vapor, slapping cheap guitars
and pitching songs into the night
like horseshoes. In his truck cab

he kept a cobalt revolver, wrapped in a red grease rag
and stuck below the driver's seat.
On the drive home, he would aim it

between passing headlights.
He'd sing into the soupy air,
his voice clear and familiar.

We Find Ourselves with Frogs

Consider frogs
as they swell with air, the injustice
they must suffer to find themselves

so suddenly large and out of text
with hunting, and all for the sake
of love song, some throaty bellow

into the midnight air. A frog's world
must be one of sudden change, expanding
the way they do to find lovers,

the quick tongue held by stones,
mouth and throat
swollen, lungs and belly a gasping

encumbrance.

The Two Directions of a Drone

spiral one

In the drainage ditch
that seeps the roadside
a sapling willow

spears the sun.
Once,
a dozen black
drones

orbited

a swarm
that weighed the willow
down into a green sea
of grasses,

swallowing the bees
and the balled limb

and now in the moment
of release,
the willow springing skyward,
a queen escapes
with a light

so like honey
that I turn my face
into the wing tips

of flight.

spiral two

Single minded flight
and the drone's affinity
to rise highest

are flowers
to the success
of the hive.
In mating

while falling

who is to say
that the embrace
of the wax moth
isn't as great

as your
touch my queen?

We are both
held
by the same lover
death, and
spiral in the breath

of loss,
liquid with the dark
drowning syrup

of flight.

Recipe for Change

Evening shadows are her dinner guests.
They fill her chairs, tucking their proper
Shoes below the table. Their appetites
Demand the simple, but tonight
She plans an exotic fare of poached chicken, garlic
And lemon rind, simmered over peppered rice.

Her mother taught her to cook, to fold napkins
And to serve from the right. Her father
Gave a swift and sober grace. Now,
Weary of recipes that appeal to the departed,
She removes their untouched plates,
Pushes them onto a shelf behind the canning jars,
And in a sauce pan, melts the silverware
Into coins for their eyes.

Cleaning Out the Garage

You discover a box of precious stones
that were gathered by your daughter at six,
rose quartz and flint and a sliver of bone,
all quarried for their intrinsic glitter.

They rival the astronomer's comet
which itself is a memory
displayed in an antique elliptical orbit
somewhere between the sun and darkness.

Burning the Beans while Meditating

It's a Zen thing the way I open one eye
and sniff the room
and then leap, run lightly on enlightened toes
towards the stove. There to find the beans
simmering into a oneness with the pot.
It's a heavy pot, a sumo pot, a cast iron stomach pot,
a pot carried by monks up Athos, a pot of hope, these beans:
Basho beans, ham'n beans, red beans and gritty rice
baked into rock in Kansas.

I spill the surface layer like acorns in a glass bowl,
charred Samadhi, sunlight on Cajun seasoning,
Buddha flower opening in thin brackish smoke,
a prayer word emptying my cabinets of spice:
oregano, cayenne, cilantro…ash

Bonnie the Clover Lady

As children we'd watch her plop her laundry basket
below the pink mimosa
and walk through the yard, soft eyed, head tilted

into invisible currents.
Knowing we watched,
she'd stoop to earth and brush her hand across the grass
as if it were a shock of hair. She might be skimming
scum from the surface of a pond,
so she could peer into the water clearly
as if it were a mirror.

Bonnie could find four leaf clovers clumped in any lawn.

They grew that way in bunches,
and where you found one, you could find two.

It was the first find that kept you hacking across the sandlot,
pressing your nose into failure.

The clover lady had the knack like few do
for seeing the ripple of four in an ocean of three.
As kids, we figured that it was a talent
coming with age, this gift
for side-stepping disappointments.

Mama DeBeauty Explains a Necessary
But Uncomfortable Aspect of Dude Ranching

Darla and Allison DeBeauty
were fine looking sisters.
They lived in the small
green rental
on Dakota Street
and never quite shut
their blinds.

I could get on Wally's
shoulders and we'd
stagger from window to
bedroom window,
hoping for a chance
to glimpse something pink.

One Sunday evening, moments
before Bonanza, Wally
caught his foot in a
gopher hole and fell against
the side of the house
so hard
it rattled the kitchen china.

Well, when Mama DeBeauty
nabbed us by the earlobes
and shook us
against the clapboard
until our gonads
rattled like little seed gourds,
I pointed to Wally
and said in shaken desperation,

"My friend's in love
with your daughter."
Well, that changed everything.
Just as quickly as Little Joe
could mount his pony,
she had us seated
in the living room
and proceeded to show us

photos of her father's
dude ranch
with stall after stall
of well mannered geldings.

Water Strider

If today I break surface tension and plunge,

it is because I have discovered the ten thousand names of love
and you have answered to them all.

So when the soft Kansas wind ripples
through yellowed leaves
the tree tops answer:

cottonwood, willow, sweet gum, elm,
cattail, blue pool,
water strider,

plunge

Vienna Sausage

Crows ride on wind. A deep strip trench cuts easterly into the earth, surrounded by shale, dumped tires, scrub sumac, scar tissue. Strip pits erupt and fold like proud flesh above a wound.

Sitting with pen and notebook, I turn my body; re-adjust my ass against the cool gray slag. Ground water seeps through my denim. Families on the way between Minden Mines and Crowburg peer at me like some carnival barker, the one who leads them into the tent with the two headed deer and the child with the white eyes.

Tomorrow, someone will push a battered car into a green pool of alkali. A plaid couch will be dumped beside the railroad tracks and burned. Teenagers will dance around it, spilling *Natural Light* and passing reefer. They will drink, cuss, and toast brotherhood in the rising sparks, the glowing coals.

Coyote tracks edge the slag pile, circling the mud, spotting the day like smudge marks, connecting the periphery where man and nightfall link arms. At midnight they are heard among the sycamores, yelping, peeling their enthusiasm for the trash lot, nosing cans of pork and beans and half eaten Vienna Sausage in wine sauce.

Voices are on the wind, somewhere with the crows. Four walnut horses with red jacketed riders appear, picking their way across the section. They weave amid the dumps and then out into the reclaimed grassland. The horses toss, pull against the reins like storms.

Game Prayer

Game Prayer

Maybe it's the way boys
look at each other before the last game,
their eyes wet and glimmering with rain.

Maybe it's that I catch them
in these shy moments of waiting,
turning the world like a pigskin,

flipping it nonchalantly, low spiral
drilling the air. Maybe it's this
moment before the splash of lights

before the game prayer
before you run from the door.
If so, forgive me

for seeing you so vulnerable,
in that quiet moment
before the helmets.

Losing Our Paychecks at Bocci Ball on V-E Day

The Italians from the mining camps
Lined the railroad ties in their baggy pants
And clean white undershirts, drinking "dago red "
From plastic cups. They hustled us with
A brash bocci ball and finessed our slender wallets
With coal darkened wagers. We were kids from town
Where the machinery for the deep shafts was built,
Where widows and daughters bought steamship tickets
For home, where their fathers had trouped
On Saturdays to trade bathtub gin for trouble.
By late evening, when the music
Began to drift down from the band dome,
They leaned on the hoods of their Fords to eye
Our bare legged girls, and grin their wide, toothy smiles.

A Kansan Visits New York City

When the neighbor's dog
barks in the rain
at the wind
in the vines of honeysuckle,
you remember the crowd
rippling down Mulberry Street
into Chinatown.
Like leaves on a fence row
they interconnect
and lace
into a rope of green,
an occasional blossom

lifting from the braid.

Coyotes

I was out trying a Volkswagen
for my daughter, when I see these two
coyotes dipping through the fence row
and tailing like two bullets of wind
across a green pasture.

I bounce behind the wheel
of this yellow bug, churning up the road's dust,
thinking thoughts of rust and end play
and new bled brakes, and I know
they never lift an eye

from my noise. Well, I'd honk
and throw a hearty wave
but the horn's dead, and the road
jogs way right
so I plow ahead, hands at ten and two,

the sudden coyotes
two specks in a farmer's field
already disappearing.

In Search of Five Mile Cave

Most of the old timers had vanished
but he had returned
to log
prize walnuts along Neosho River bottom.
He spoke of a cave
in some seldom seen hollow
where his father
had once lost a dog,
and of walking
with lantern and gun until sunrise,
hurrying behind his father's boots
in search of the favored hound
who in chasing a coon to ground
had slipped in on greater night,
his baying shrinking faster
than their lamps could follow.

Hunting the Oldest Grave in the Town Cemetery

was acclaimed as one among many
great history lessons,
completed by the third grade class
during the Kansas Centennial.
The class waded among headstones
drowned in fescue
and crawled below the junipers to etch
newsprint with charcoal.
Classmates visited the old fort,
and balanced on the ramparts,
catching the faraway cries of stragglers
from the skirmish on Cow Creek. Others
in tilling the garden
turned horseshoes between Tom's tomatoes,
unearthing a bit more
of the Iowa City blacksmith.
North at the natural ford,
some searched the unplowed pastures
for buffalo wallows and military trail wagon ruts.
The class dug a hole below the flagpole
and planted a time capsule
with their full names signed in pencil
on a scroll of Big Chief.
They would each be one hundred
and nine when they dug it up,
except for the new kid from Missouri
who'd been held back a grade.
He'd be one hundred and ten.

Shooting the Snapper

The first sun snags him
like a fishing line, netting his soup bowl
shell, his razor claws,
his slate eyes peering
with dim curiosity down
his queer, hooked snout.
He waits, a phalanx, beside the flood brush,
a guardian of prehistoric DNA.

When the Crawford boys stop their pickup
and pull a .22 from behind the seat,
he doesn't edge into the bean rows
but rises on powerful, bowed legs,
suddenly all piss and spit. The boys
circle to within a few steps, aiming deep
into his bone encased brain.

His leathered neck strains
with the one plan decoded. Hissing
at the leveled blue barrel,
he snaps beautifully at
the exploding sun.

The Last Bones of Mine Creek

after Ken Burns

We find in the annals of historians
pioneer photographers, catching
battle on glass negatives.

They brave wild musket shot,
by planting themselves behind wooden boxes
like apple saplings, gathering light

from Lawrence or Lone Jack or West Port,
gingerly storing battle cry between sheets
of newsprint, frail and thin as windows.

Not unlike a soldier turned farmer,
photographs find their way
into the skylights of greenhouses.

The pellucid gardenia, the limpid azalea
push fleshy limbs into
the wounds of battle dead,

poppy eyes, periwinkle mouths,
rose tongues swollen with unspoken
poetry, bleached

by the sun into transparency.
The last bones of Mine Creek
are ghosts above clay pots,

the potter's small shovel
turning mounds of rich soil:
potash, bitterroot, bone meal.

The Oxbow

The old woman has oxbowed,
    weathered
        and turned back upon herself
            like a slowly drying stream.
              Today, she sits at a small table
                in a large room, and listens to herself

            tell secrets. Her most important visitors
        are the departed
    who return
        upon mysterious invitation,
            rising from the fathoms of her past

              like catfish
           in turbid pools, waiting
        the autumn rains
     that will again
  connect them
to the river.

Hiking with the Cedar Children

The children ran through the woods
without concern, the path back to the car
a matter they left to the wind.

I kept distance
so they'd find the sun splattering

unhindered through yellowed oaks,
the squawk of jays
exotic as macaws,

and the stones of the footpath
steps into twilight.
How could I interrupt

unless it were to parcel out sunflower seeds
or snap a fallen limb into a walking stick,
the weight of my foot as sure

as the moss
that maps the north side.

Rappelling Out of El Ojo Del Gato in Cloud Cover

There was a night when the wind blew,
blew so hard the blinds straightened
and fell, and I awoke to find you gone
and the child in myself missing.

Odd, how even in The Eye of the Cat
I think of you, the Gulf
having turned the coast into a bowl
of gray, the cold wind
sending wisps of rain and swirls of darkened dust
into this hole on the cliff.
Here, where bones left by wide winged hawks
crack below my feet, we shiver
in waiting our turn for the next leap.
In the dark *Eye*
the rope is a single assurance
that the attraction
of gravity
draws me towards you.

For as I fall back
along the ragged scree,
I control the tug of rack
and slide of nylon.
I double check the locking nut, the
hold of harness, the looped bowline,
and step off into free air.

I drop from *The Eye of the Cat*
into clouds, the thin *Blue Water*
calling into the distance
like a lover,
who in communicating
less and less
vanishes without belay.

Satori in a Village in Old Mexico

You ask me if I can smell the prayer in cooking
in the smoke of the sidewalk enchiladas,
grilled chicken, onions on charcoal.

I half expect to see Francis
hobbling across the plaza on bare feet, Clare beside him.
Their eyes somewhere off beyond the church
and the incredulous Brother Leo. Somewhere off
beyond the vows

in the sunlight
where the song of the bluebird begins.

"How Saint Anthony Converted the Heretics
By Preaching to Fishes"

after The Little Flowers

Standing on the banks between the river
and the sea, Anthony began to call the fishes.
He must have admired their calm,
seeing how they rose to the surface,
eyes lucid as the water, swimming
with others of their kind, small fish
to the shallow water and larger fish
to the deeper.
Look how they wait a bit out of water
like rows of piano keys,
stirred by their longing to be played,
each word a fingertip on the head of a fish.
See how they sink when touched,
a musical note dropping into the depths
where others of their kind
stir in quiet schools, listening.

The Day Before Winter

Leaves scatter in tight winds
while the grackle sketches a bouncing line
across the picket fence
to a place on the lawn.

There is little movement,
even among the neighbors,
who may with long, November chins
dropped to their chests
wedge a foot into the back door
and with a tip of a broom

sweep yesterday down the steps.

Reading to Her Daughter

Hunting New Cave on Cecil Creek

Along the road that leads to Cecil Creek,
the black limbed fingers of maples, oaks and elms
stretch map-like into the stony silence.

If a man follows them, then he follows himself
to where a blackbird flies the dome of winter sky,
the rush of wind through wing feathers

as hushed as limestone,
gray, solid as the quiet within.

Wintered Bat at John Eddy Cave

Slick with water beads the bat
turns circles in the chamber's back
reaches. The darting turns that twist
the very air in blackness burst

into the flashlight's beam.
He pinwheels the cave's fracture, the seam
of vault and crevice
a blacker night than midnight's darkness.

And here, the winged fury
brushes with acrobatic surety
the new moon of my face
and disappears, apart, unabased

through whorls of stone and Ozark mud.
As such, the lone bat is understood,
swallowed in his solitude
a single heart beating single blood.

Some Moments Are Frozen

The sun's finally out, but between
the fallen crocus and the trash truck
are thousands of twinkling ice
crystals. I'm fixing the bird
feeder, restringing a nylon cord
to the sawed-off limb, letting the
weight of the seed pull it taut
to where it pendulums in the wind
of sparrows. Nothing in this moment
lends itself to words.
Even if I had waited a lifetime
no one would speak.
The neighbor lady would pull
shut her curtains before noon
and the dog would sit sullenly
in the flower bed, her head
like a spade
raised over the dark soil.

Muskrat Dump

The afternoon sunlight
warms my back
while woodpeckers drum
hollow limbs in the tree
tangled dumps. A few
remaining persimmons
darken. Wind rustles
the brown undergrowth;
leaves clatter and snag
on bunch berry vines.
I lay among them like
a branch, fallen
and comfortable with decay.

The pit's green water
crests a canoe, red keel
creasing the surface
like the snout of a muskrat
stretching for the coal slag
shoreline. Overhead
the blue sky is interrupted
only by thoughts
of sleep,
and amazingly, out
of the scrub oak
a December butterfly,
as fragile and temporary as daylight.

Walking Pine Creek in Winter

The stones, bleached white, capsize the sun
turn the creek silver, a wrinkled cellophane
current, running from leaking cap rock

to a river miles through pines. If you kick
over stones with your boot, you'll find the undersides
white as well. So great the spring turbulence

that the streambed itself is turned,
rolled again and again into the light of the sun.
Somewhat like a truth about yourself

that you've hoped to avoid,
hidden like a nail shell or crawdad claw,
turned and overturned

with bleached river stone, your corners and crannies
smoothed and polished, there is
no shadow for secret, just simple sunlight

bending simple truth from your bones.

The Something Above Which We Share Below

When they painted the mortuary ceiling,
Mr. Lemon wheeled out the only body
and plastic was laid from corner
to red carpeted corner. Each ceiling
tile was removed and handed down
from workman to workman,
dusted, stain stopped,
and a slick white latex rolled.
By the time the last tile was painted
the first was dry
and so they went back
up *click click click*
like pieces in a rather elementary puzzle.
When completed, the plastic
was wadded into a large ball
and tossed into an alley bin.
Then Mr. Lemon wheeled back in
the only body. It's single lapel carnation
as white as the white of the ceiling above.

How Wally Lost His Thumb
and the Boy Scouts Became Cannibals

We had fought
for hours over the
cooking of the stew,
wrestling in the yellow
hay like denim clad
cubs. Until Wally
in a fit of ambition
whittled a chunk
from his favorite thumb.
It was a masterful cleave
with a well-whetted blade
and an inspirational heave

that chucked the thumb
thick into the pan
of sizzling ham,
where as quickly as spit
it curled and fizzled
into an unidentifiable
hunk of gristle

awfully comparable
to dinner.
So of course here lay
the quandary:
to dismiss the ham
into the autumn turned leaves
or let it all fry
down into the sumptuous
fat we'd planned.

Amid curled pork,
slices of onion, potatoes
and sliver of thumb,
a dozen eggs were dumped,
and when at last
the plates were mopped
and the spatula cleaned,

the thumb
garnished with salt
and a little pepper

had been nibbled down
or swallowed whole.
From that day on
it became apparent
a cannibal was among us
a boy scout within us.

Double Dating with Wally

Well, he was smart.
He understood his role.
He'd tell girls flat, I'm everything
you were ever
warned about in Driver's Ed.
I drink and smoke and show
off in intersections,
race trains, do donuts,
and refuse to yield
the right-of-way.
I'm a son of a bitch at the wheel
and seldom in touch
with reality.

Well, the girls would start
screaming and begging him to stop
but Wally was off,
blown into one of those crazy moods
to which he was prone,
what with homegrown and malt
and females pretending to be helpless,
so it all added up
to burying the speedometer
in the scream of the road,
beating a lucky guess
through Five Mile Corner
and yelping out of the window
like he was calling to the moon.

Eventually, he'd stop, pull
off roadside and want to know
what all the fuss was about,
and the girls would say you're
crazy crazy crazy
and we're getting out so we
can live a while longer.
And Wally would sadden and promise,
really promise to drive like he cared.
Because he was wrong and sorry
and his little brother was all crippled and
lived in a wheelchair and could
only put picture puzzles into whole pictures.

So they'd feel something sorry and stay
and he'd kick it
back into gear and tear ninety
towards Columbus, following
Highway 7 towards the horizon line,
laughing and laughing like he was
crazy crazy crazy,
and they'd cry, pounding on his arm,
you promised you wouldn't,
you promised.

The Great Night with Rednecks

Edward was in love
with fun and when
Wally threw him
onto the floor of the
Sad Song Bar, he kicked the tip
of his western boot
into Wally's groin.
Wally crumpled into
the lap of Junior Ash.
Junior yelled fag, threw
a bottle at one of
the laughing Simpson brothers
and clipped a redneck
they called Ace.

At that point Sally Ann screamed
fingers got smashed, cheeks
gashed and one girl
had her bra unsnapped.
When the bouncers elbowed
Charlotte into a balcony post,

Ace lost his mind and
ground one gorilla into the floor boards.
The other was
stuffed in a urinal
by a crowd chanting, "We love Ace."
So really, nothing was unusual
with the *Sad Song* crowd.

Later, when the sheriff showed
and unloaded a round of tear gas
through the windows,
Edward and Wally cried,
but not for lack of fun.

Anything for Susie

When I was four
this lovely girl combed
her golden hair against
her red lapel,

stroked it in place
with her palm, while asking me
in the same breath to crawl
into Splinter's plywood

dog house. I did.
I climbed inside, not knowing why,
snagging my cap on nails, pushing my
hands through the mildewed

dog pissy straw. As soon
as my feet cleared the sill,
she slapped the door shut, shoved
out the light, and latched me in

with the spiders and the fleas.
When I rattled the door,
she giggled. When I kicked
with the heels of my new

western boots, she laughed,
and when I cried, she said
ok baby wait a minute
and she jiggled the latch.

When I quieted, wiped
away the tears and snot with a sleeve,
she cracked the door
and her demon dog Splinters

bolted in, chasing
circles around my face,
my hands whirling, winnowing
the straw. The dust rose in my throat,

a gag that I hocked
but forced myself to swallow,
rather than spit
on a dog who deserved it.

Puttering

dissolves into the soil.
The hat on the fencepost
slouches in
the midnight rain
like a dream
collapsed
and fallen in.
The brim is
permanently funneled,
a rain spout
above the herb garden.
The maze of bricks
lifted from the patio,
reset
in the circular whirl
of a wheel;
cilantro, comfrey,
chamomile,
spin outwards
away from the bird-
bath hub.
Even our footprints
dissolve like the summer,
the crows
thieves in the corn.

Copperhead

The woman herds
a single cow
through pasture
that's mostly nettles
and sun-baked rock.
Startled by the fall
of her boot, the copperhead
streaks the curve of her leg.
Strikes.
The dog yelps
and begins to run in circles.
She hikes her sunflower dress,
and lifts her leg
into the air.
The snake
dangles from her calve.
She feels
the muscle in him,
the tug of his gravity.
The cow turns dumbly,
bell clacking.

The woman spins,
snake extending, stretching
like a bolo as she whirls,
jaws locked,
fangs loosened in
slender tracks.
She jigs. Kicks.
The snake
flips
over a fence post and skids
to the water's edge.
The dog leaps and snarls,
skittering backwards
until his hind legs
slide into the creek.
When finally, there
is no room for retreat,
he paws the gravel
and dips his head
in fits
of remarkable
barking.

75

The Night of Bacon and Baseball

When the wind blew the power lines
Into the shelter house, it showered the park
With pigeon feathers. Sparks popped
And snapped and the smell of cooked bird
Rose with the blue smoke into the light poles.
Of course, all was pitched
Into darkness, and the boys playing baseball
Began to slide into whatever base
Was closest. An old woman frying bacon
On Martin Street cursed her new electric stove
And wished her son had never insisted
On the change from gas. The bacon
Bubbled and sizzled down in the heated grease
Until it was somewhat cooked, but she
Tossed it angrily into the trash. Finally,
Lightning cracked and the boys on the ball diamond
Were hurried into the dugouts by the coaches
Where they sat with their gloves on their laps
Swinging their legs and watching the field
Disappear in a torrent of rain. Two teenagers
Who had escaped the bleachers and slipped
Into a Ford Taurus saw this as an opportunity
To unleash zippers and buttons. Fast Ernie,
The dog, stretched on his hind legs
To nose the bacon from the trash can,
The rain water streaming down his back
In freshets of grime and fleas. The electric company
Had a truck on the way, two workers,
One of them smoking a cigar, the other tuning
The Royals game on the radio. Cats skulked
In the shrubs for the rain to let up.
They licked their lips and sharpened their claws.

Maybe if Kafka

had invented the Frisbee,
instead of the safety helmet,
he would have liked dogs.
Maybe, the story would have had
Gregor and his dog
leaping,
spinning the disc
and laughing at spring's
bright existential spin,

and his sister, Grete,
beauty that she is in gray,
how much more in yellow
would she have
enticed the very air
with her sweet violin,

and dared this day,
her first day,
to crack a window,
to consider that the grubby
cockroach feet
crawling to embrace the sill
are attached to wings?

Make Believe Indian Love Poem

When I emerge from the last smoky kiva,
I will find you there, old woman. Our possessions
wrapped in buffalo hide and lashed

to a travois I will help you pull.
Even to the mountain of storms on the blue mesa,
our breath clouds mixing in the chill dawn,

the rainbow I followed as a boy
still in your eyes.

Where a deer fell

my daughter uncovers bones,
overgrown with briar, glued to soil
by leaf meal and frost.
The forest floor clings as
we lift the skull into light, examining the
little spirit that remains,
the brittle nostrils opened to wind, the eyes filled
with the shadows of small ponds.

Shoots of honeysuckle, green briar and grape,
a tendril of ivy and finger of mandrake
push through the spinal canal, separate
vertebrae, disjoin knee from shank and hip from thigh,
encircle a bleached jaw, tie the toothy
mandible like stone to earth, lacing the caved ribs
with vine, pulling the whitened
bones into flesh.

Reading to Her Daughter

The song of rivers is the voice of a woman
who in reading a book to her daughter
resonates with the melody of water.
She creates words the way
waterfowl fly, soft wings
fluttering in her mouth, sentences
streaming to become rivers.

Her daughter listens, and in the end
will touch her fingers to her mother's lips
like a willow twig dragging current,
language breaking around her,
tumbling calmly into the eddy of the room,
where awash in words, they swim the evening.

Al Ortolani was born in Huntington, New York and grew up in Pittsburg, Kansas. He was educated at Pittsburg State University and for the past 37 years has taught at Kansas schools in Baxter Springs, Pittsburg and Overland Park (Blue Valley) as well as an adjunct at Pittsburg State University. He has worked as a house painter, chimney sweep, antique dealer, juvenile counselor, pony handler, canoeing instructor, gas station attendant and soda jerk. He once claimed to have cooked the best bowl of chili in the state of Kansas. Al Ortolani is presently co-editor of *The Little Balkans Review.*

The tighter you squeeze, the less you have.

—Thomas Merton

www.ingramcontent.com/pod-product-compliance
Lightning Source LLC
Chambersburg PA
CBHW051845040426
42447CB00006B/703